Born in Regina, Saskatchewan, in 1952, Robert Clinton has lived most of his life in the Canadian West and currently resides in Edmonton, Alberta. A graduate of the National Theatre School of Canada, he has performed in over fifty productions as a member of Canadian Actor's Equity and ACTRA. A six-time winner of first prize in the Alberta Playwriting Competition, he began playwriting by staging four of his works at Edmonton's Fringe Festival. His other plays include *Mirage, Man in the Jungle, Editing Suite,* and *The Honeymoon Boy. The Mail Order Bride* premiered at Theatre Network in Edmonton and has been produced by the Blyth Festival and Prairie Theatre Exchange in Winnipeg.

*The Mail Order Bride*
*By Robert Clinton*

**BLIZZARD PUBLISHING**
Winnipeg • Niagara Falls

First published 1989 in Canada and the United States by
Blizzard Publishing Inc.
73 Furby Street, Winnipeg, Canada R3C 2A2.
Reprinted 1991, 1999

Distributed in the United States by General Distribution Services,
4500 Witmer Industrial Estates, Niagara Falls, NY 14305-1386.

Cover design by Terry Gallagher.
Printed for Blizzard Publishing in Canada.

5   4   3

Blizzard Publishing gratefully acknowledges the support of
Canadian Heritage, the Manitoba Arts Council, and the Canada
Council to its publishing program.

Cataloguing in Publication Data

Clinton, Robert Mitchell, 1952–
The mail order bride
   A play.
   ISBN: 0-921368-09-7
I. Title.
PS8555.L568M3 1989  C812/.54  C89-098140-X
PR9199.3.C546M3 1989

*This play is dedicated to my parents, Irene and Leslie.*
*They have always given me the best example.*

# Acknowledgements

*The Mail Order Bride* had a three-year genesis. It won two first prizes in the Alberta Playwriting competition, received four workshops, and grew from three five-minute radio dramas, to a one-act with songs, to a full-length play. Many talented people are part of her. Greg Rogers, Darlene Bradley, Jack Ackroyd, CBC Radio Calgary, Apple Macintosh®, Kevin Smith, Michael Becker, the Edmonton Fringe Festival, Stephen Heatley, Alberta Playwright's Network, Greg Dowler-Coltman, Theatre Network, the Canada Council, Earl Klein, Christine McInnis, Nola Auguston, Eric Kramer, Warren Hartman, Michael Murdock, Judy Mahbey, Kent Gallie, Kate Newby, Weston McMillan, Susan Sneath, the Blyth Festival, Jerry Franken, Judith Orban, Ron Gabriel, Nancy Roberts, Bill Dunlop, Greg Spottiswood, Bridget O'Sullivan, Lorna Wilson, Katherine Kaszas, the Alberta Government Department of Culture and Multiculturalism, Alberta Theatre Projects, Craig Davidson, Marion Muroney, Bruce Parkhouse, Maureen Thomas, Howie Segal, Paul Cowling, Ellen Rae Hennesy, Allan McInnis, Randy Jenne, Bill Dow, Vaughn Fuford, Carol Sinclair, Peter Smith, Aidan Devine, and Karen Barker. And T.G. and Django. And Gordon and Peter.

—Robert Clinton

*The Mail Order Bride* was first produced at Theatre Network, Edmonton, Alberta, on April 21, 1988, with the following cast:

| | |
|---|---|
| HAROLD ENGLISH | Michael Murdock |
| CHARLOTTE TEETER-EMERY | Judy Mahbey |
| ART MILLIGAN | Kent Gallie |
| RACHEL TEETER | Kate Newby |
| CHARLES TEETER | Weston McMillan |
| RUSSELL TEETER | David Mann |
| EVA TEETER | Susan Sneath |

Directed by Stephen Heatley
and Greg Dowler-Coltman
Dramaturged by Warren Hartman
Sound design by Michael Becker
Lighting design by Ruth Lysak-Martynkiw
Costume design by Daniel VanHeist
Set design by Morris Ertman
Stage Manager: Terri Gillis

## *Playwright's Note*

Plays are meant to be figured out in rehearsal and performed—a puzzle and a blueprint. There are few guides for the reader except problems posed to those with weeks of rehearsal and many readings.

Programme notes *must* include a character list and descriptions. Eva is pronounced "Ava," Krysa is pronounced "Chris-ah," "…" and "—" are different. Some dates have a plus-or-minus factor of about four years. Survey stakes are metre-long steel rods. (It is illegal to remove them. Many farmers pushed them into the ground and farmed over them.) All silences are not created equal. These are neither nice people nor do they get happy endings. Always make the choice that hurts the most—either hurts another character or hurts your own. There's lots of room for selfishness. Nice will take care of itself. In this play.

## Characters

HAROLD ENGLISH: A crazy coot.

CHARLOTTE EMERY-TEETER: A mail order bride.

ART MILLIGAN: A travelling salesman.

RACHEL TEETER: A farmer's daughter.

CHARLES TEETER: A farmer.

RUSSELL TEETER: A hot-shot pilot.

EVA TEETER: A young mother.

## Time and Place

1954
(1908, 1916, 1918, 1924, 1941, 1952)
The Teeter family farm.

# Act One

*(House lights, work lights on. Preparations for the play. HAROLD starts early.)*

HAROLD: We still got five? We're not starting yet. Lemme know when you're ready, [Stage Manager's name]. Stage Manager. Tells us what to do. You too. I've got time to get some more flowers? *(Leaves, returns.)* Name's Harold. Halfa sec'.

*(HAROLD leaves, comes back with a pallet of bedding plants, lunch bucket, legal-size envelope, bedding tools. He sprinkles dirt on the envelope.)*

Gotta get this thing jes so. We'll be ready t' go in a minute. This is my favorite part of the show. They let me come out early. If they didn't I told 'em I'd change the ending. Started doin' this a few years ago. I'm just about retired, guess I can't give it all up. This set is supposed to be the old Teeter place. Don't look like the real thing, but it'll change. So will I. Sometimes I'll look like this. *(His expression doesn't change.)* Sometimes like this. And, this. Didn't notice anything? The other actors'll be out soon, you just play along. That's my place down there, you can see almost all of it. From up here you can see the whole District. This ain't much of a hill but there's horizon all around. Nothin' to get in the way of the view. Flat. All the way to the edge. Pretty ain't it? *(Pause.)* It's an acquired taste.

*(Worklights begin going out.)*

I'm getting ahead of myself. More people are going to come out. Some of 'em are going to be real and some of them aren't. Well, they're all real but some of 'em are only real to me and some're … Let's just start.

*(Blackout. Music. Prairie sunrise to prairie morning.)*

*(Gives the real time.)* Time to go to work. Nothin' up my sleeve. Company's comin' today and I haveta get these flowers in before day after tomorrow. Spring jumped up early a week ago, and these guys are used to bein' out. Get 'em in before it's too late. An odd bunch. All of 'em grow wild around here. It's hard t' tell which is which when they're just little guys. I can 'cause I planted 'em, so I know that much: how well the plants they came from did, what the books say. Who knows how it's gonna turn out, but the overview helps. Cause 'n' effect. What makes 'em what they are. Imagine seein' all that. I mean, for us, eh?

> *(Music.)*

That whole chain of stuff, all the choices 'n' mistakes. It's there. It all happened. Maybe we could sorta let ourselves see it? *(Silence.)* I can. See it, but sometimes I miss it lookin' at stuff I already know.

> *(CHARLOTTE comes out of the house. In her mid-fifties. She carries a note.)*

CHARLOTTE: Harold.

HAROLD: She isn't the company. She's not real. *(As a teenager.)* Mrs. Teeter?

CHARLOTTE: Where's my husband?

HAROLD: He's helpin' my dad with the—

CHARLOTTE: I shall have to tell him.

HAROLD: Halfa sec' an' I'll drive you.

CHARLOTTE: The train left forty-five minutes ago. She's gone.

> *(CHARLOTTE walks off down the yard.)*

HAROLD: That lady died last week. The whole District came out. That was her in the middle of the twenties. She changed a lot since then.

> *(A hot afternoon. ART hurries up to the house.)*

She, ah, before that, she changed a lot, too … ah. Cause 'n effect.

> *(ART knocks on the door.)*

… y' see, the people comin' today? They're the—

> *(ART knocks on the door.)*

ART: Let's get moving!

HAROLD: … halfa sec' …

> *(RACHEL steps out of the house. A teenager. Dressed for travel. She carries a small suitcase.)*

This won't take long.

RACHEL: We'd better hurry.

>  *(RACHEL and ART leave.)*

HAROLD: When they wanna come back there's no stoppin' them. Things didn't happen in that order. That was the same day when you met Mrs. Teeter, the day after the Harvest Party.

>  *(A drunken song. CHARLES staggers up to the house. Middle aged.)*

… this is no way to meet this man. This happened the same day. That night, actually. Do you think there's a pattern here?

CHARLES: Harold?

HAROLD: Yesir Mr. Teeter.

CHARLES: I told you: Charlie.

HAROLD: Yesir.

CHARLES: Harold. Do you know what this is?

HAROLD: What is?

CHARLES: *(Including everything.)* This is.

HAROLD: No sir.

CHARLES: This is it.

HAROLD: …?

CHARLES: Y' c'n only dream of this. Everything off early. Decent prices for once. Ya watch … hope it'll all line up …

HAROLD: That's real nice.

CHARLES: Y' can't argue with that.

HAROLD: Best in the District.

>  *(CHARLES goes into the house.)*

CHARLES: … my bins are full of rats …

>  *(A screen door slams.)*

HAROLD: … ah, not really his best moment. None of ours, actually. Ya coulda met 'em at so many better times. *(Pause.)* That's just about everybody. Except fer … Rachel? That girl with the suitcase? She had a brother but you won't see him. Neither can I. He was gone more than he was ever here, 'n' that was the most important thing about him.

>  *(The sound of a sportscar driving up a gravel road.)*

That'll be the last two. These are the real people. That's why they have a car noise. I'm supposed to be plantin' these flowers when they get here. This is 1954. Pretty, isn't it. Well, not yet, it's just comin' up. Western Red Lily. "Lillium Philadelphicum." Some folks call 'em Prairie or Tiger Lilies. Used to be able to find these all over the place but so many folks pick 'em 'n try t' take 'em home.

*(During HAROLD's botany lesson, RUSSELL walks up the yard. Reflective aviator shades.)*

RUSSELL: Great. *(Step creaks underfoot.)* Somebody'd break their neck. Everything's still here. Damn. Hasn't been painted since the thirties.

HAROLD: 1941. A year before your grandfather died.

*(Silence.)*

RUSSELL: You've got the papers.

HAROLD: Over there.

*(Silence.)*

RUSSELL: I have to see them.

HAROLD: Help yerself.

*(A legal-size envelope covered with dirt.)*

RUSSELL: Country living.

HAROLD: Where you come from this mornin'?

RUSSELL: The city. Nearest good hotel.

HAROLD: Y' musta been really bootin' 'er.

RUSSELL: Is everything on this list here?

HAROLD: Which one?

RUSSELL: Pink.

HAROLD: Who knows.

RUSSELL: I beg your pardon?

HAROLD: That's from the Insurance Company. It's forty years old. Big company bought 'em out ten years ago an' never checked up.

RUSSELL: What about the yellow one?

HAROLD: No one knows about that one either.

RUSSELL: Is there a list of the household contents?

HAROLD: Don't worry about that.

RUSSELL: Where is it?

HAROLD: There isn't one. I told ya not t' worry.

RUSSELL: Why didn't someone go through this?

HAROLD: Yer Grandad didn't need lists. Besides, the will says a member of the family's got to.

RUSSELL: All this should have been taken care of!

HAROLD: I don't think either of 'em were plannin' on dyin'.

(*Silence.*)

RUSSELL: Eva. Eva!

EVA: *(Downhill.)* Hold on.

RUSSELL: Time's a wasting! Where's the phone?

HAROLD: Disconnected 'er last week.

RUSSELL: Damn. Eva!

(*EVA comes up the hill. She carries small flowers. Simultaneous conversations.*)

EVA: I picked flowers.

HAROLD: Crocuses.

EVA: They're so delicate.

HAROLD: They been up since before melt. "Anemone patens."

EVA: I could hardly see them.

HAROLD: Kinda pale. Tough to see against dead grass.

EVA: They aren't very impressive, are they?

HAROLD: They are, they just ain't big.

RUSSELL: *(Complete overlap through the above conversation.)* We've got to get organized. You start with the house. Make a list of as much of the crap in there as you can. I'll get this stuff checked. There's twice as much here. This won't get done by itself. Listen!

(*RUSSELL walks EVA a few paces.*)

There is a lot of work to get done if we're going to be back in four days.

EVA: I'm sure you'll make up time on the way.

RUSSELL: We're ahead of schedule, let's not lose that.

EVA: Then you can schedule a chance to recover from your driving.

RUSSELL: I didn't suggest taking the car out here.

EVA: Even so, you're having such fun.

RUSSELL: This is business time!

EVA: *(The crocuses.)* For you, Mr. Assistant V.P.

(*Silence. RUSSELL doesn't take the small flowers.*)

RUSSELL: We'll get started? *(To HAROLD.)* You take this list and mark off anything that isn't on the—

HAROLD: Has to be a member of the family.

RUSSELL: You can't expect me—! There must be two hundred things here!

HAROLD: I'm workin'.

*(Silence.)*

RUSSELL: Where's the stuff on this one.

HAROLD: Geeze. Could be anywhere. Some'll be in the machine shed. Prob'ly find mosta this stuff in the barn. 'Cept the old Ford flat-bed. Mrs. Teeter lent it to Juke Lessard last winter to haul pigs.

RUSSELL: Didn't he bring it back?

HAROLD: He got drunk and drove it through the ice on his dugout.

RUSSELL: So the rest of this is—?!

HAROLD: His prize sow Buttercup got frostbit swimmin' out.

*(Silence.)*

RUSSELL: I'll be in the barn. Maybe you can get started on the house?

EVA: In a minute.

HAROLD: Auction's tomorrow.

RUSSELL: I know!

HAROLD: The revised list's gotta be at their office over in Leaver by closing tonight or they'll postpone it 'til next week.

RUSSELL: Don't you think it's time we—?!

EVA: I'm catching my breath.

HAROLD: The wreckin' crew's comin' in day after tomorrow, so ya can't cancel.

RUSSELL: *(The bedding plants.)* If they're coming then why …? Never mind. Let's see some hustle!

*(RUSSELL leaves. EVA throws flowers after him. Silence.)*

EVA: … sorry …

HAROLD: Huh? Oh, that's okay. It's rough when yer Gran' dies.

EVA: It's been a long trip.

HAROLD: Come from back East, eh?

EVA: Two and a half days.

HAROLD: Good time.

EVA: Not for him.

HAROLD: I don't know anybody who's made it that far in two days.

EVA: It's … very tiring. Marry a pilot and you marry his driving.

HAROLD: Prob'ly get used to it after a while.

EVA: Ten years.

HAROLD: Oh. Didja bring the kids?

EVA: He's with friends. Russell didn't think …

> *(Silence.)*

HAROLD: What's his name?

EVA: Paul. Fourteen months.

HAROLD: 'At's nice.

> *(Silence.)*

That's some slick little car. Prob'ly bought that in Europe, eh?

EVA: Boys must have toys.

HAROLD: Y' should stop at the service station before y' go. The fellas'a never seen anythin' like that.

EVA: Great. Now it's bound to break down. Strand us in the … wherever this is.

HAROLD: Here? This is right in the middle. Where y' always been.

EVA: *(Silence.)* It's been a long mor—

HAROLD: Look around.

EVA: … it's just horizon.

HAROLD: There y' are. Right in the middle. Only here y' can really see it.

EVA: Yes, but I've never been here before. I don't know where I am.

HAROLD: The centre part's the same.

EVA: I've never been to this pla—

HAROLD: If y' know yer way 'round that, then wherever y' go, at least y' know where y' are.

> *(Silence.)*

EVA: You're crazy.

HAROLD: That's what it says in the program.

EVA: What are you doing here? Do you live here?

HAROLD: 'At's my place down there. I'm just cleanin' up. Seein' who comes by.

EVA: Many people?

HAROLD: Four just before you pulled up.

EVA: Oh. I guess she was important out here. People coming to pay their last respects.

HAROLD: Got lotsa telegrams but didn't have nowhere to send 'em. Was real hard gettin' hold a' yer husband.

EVA: *(Silence.)* We moved.

HAROLD: Had to try him after we found out his mother was somewhere in …

EVA: The Belgian Congo.

HAROLD: Imagine someone born here bein' over there.

EVA: She asked Russell to come out and take care of the estate. We got her telegram three days ago and he couldn't very well…. She wants everyone to know she's sorry she can't be here.

HAROLD: I'm sure they'll all appreciate it.

EVA: I'll tell her you said that, Mr.—We haven't even introduced ourselves. Please excuse me.

HAROLD: Sure thing Eva.

EVA: You know my name?

HAROLD: Russell's mother sent some letters. Two I think. Besides, he was screamin' it loud enough to hear in town. I'm Harold English. Spelt like the language.

EVA: I'm pleased to meet you Mr. English.

HAROLD: Harold.

>    *(Shake hands. EVA's hand gets dirty.)*

Sorry 'bout that. *(Gives kerchief.)* Just a little manoor.

EVA: So. You knew Russell's grandparents?

>    *(Music.)*

HAROLD: *(A take on the music.)* Must be a leading question.

EVA: If you'd rather I didn't ask …?

HAROLD: No, no, that's fine. Good a place as any. Yep. I've known the Teeter family since I was born.

EVA: That long?

HAROLD: It ain't that long.

EVA: No, I didn't mean—

HAROLD: I'm only eighteen. This is all mileage.

EVA: *(Smiling.)* Mr. Eng—!

HAROLD: Yes, I knew'em a long time.

EVA: And Mrs. Teeter, she was …?

HAROLD: Eighty-four.

EVA: I can't imagine living that long.

HAROLD: I'm goin' for it.

EVA: That'd be just … just too much living.

HAROLD: She started a whole new life when she was older'n you. She was a mail order bride.

EVA:—? Russell's grandmother?!

HAROLD: She came out here with eleven other ladies. 1908. Middla winter. Twelve men from the District got together and sent off for 'em.

EVA: How embarassing!

HAROLD: She shoulda felt ashamed for bein' sent for?

EVA: For being bought.

HAROLD: That didn't make her a worse mother.

*(Winter and a cold wind. Movement inside the house.)*

EVA: Well, I don't know what it was like back then.

HAROLD: Same as now. Y' shoulda known her.

*(CHARLOTTE comes out of the house. She carries a suitcase and a coat.)*

CHARLOTTE: Harold?

HAROLD: Yes?

CHARLOTTE: This is all going to the rummage sale, if you want to go through it, see if there's anything …

HAROLD: Sure.

CHARLOTTE: … it's a mess up there …

HAROLD: She'd drive y' 'round the bend, straightenin' everythin'.

CHARLOTTE: … his things everywhere … *(The coat.)* I know I threw this out.

HAROLD: Mr. Teeter was a real pack rat. Tried to save everythin'.

CHARLOTTE: I wore this the day I met him.

*(Winter wind. CHARLES crosses the yard. Middle aged.)*

CHARLES: What the hell are you doin'?!

HAROLD: Comin' t' help.

CHARLES: It's cold enough to freeze a horse fart to the barn door!

HAROLD: But you said you want—

CHARLES: Four bloody o'clock in the afternoon and it's sunset! It's only January 27. There's two months left! This place ain't fit fer— Is that what day it is?

HAROLD: What's left of it.

CHARLES: Damn.

EVA: They mustn't have had an easy life out here.

HAROLD: Here, there, it's the same.

CHARLES: Twenty-five years. Y'd think I'd remember. I can still get her somethin'. I'm goin' into town.

CHARLOTTE: Thirty-five anniversaries.

CHARLES: Y' got any money?

>*(Far away sound of a steam locomotive. CHARLES waits at a railway station.)*

HAROLD: In the winter of 1908 she quit work, got on a train full of strangers, and came out here to meet the stranger she was gonna marry.

>*(The train slows, blows whistles, and comes to a stop. The train hisses steam, bells ring, passengers pass by throughout.)*

CONDUCTOR (HAROLD): Mid-ling! All out for the town of Mid-ling! Ten minute stop!

>*(CHARLES searches among the women descending from the train.)*

CHARLES: *(Mispronounces.)* Miss Emery? Oh, sorry. 'Scuse me, are you Miss Emery? Are you Miss Emery? … you neither, eh?

>*(CHARLOTTE steps down from the train.)*

CHARLOTTE: Excuse me? Excuse me …? Mr. ah … Mr. Teeter?

CHARLES: Yeah?

CHARLOTTE: It's me. I'm her.

CHARLES: Eh?

CHARLOTTE: Charlotte "Emery." The Agency …? You wrote to me?

CHARLES: Yeah.

>*(Silence.)*

CHARLOTTE: Shall I …?

>*(She gestures to her heavy bag and the distance between them.)*

Or will you …?

CHARLES: Huh? Oh …

>*(CHARLES moves to her. Silence.)*

CHARLOTTE: It's nice to finally meet yo—

CHARLES: Your picture was different.

CHARLOTTE: … I assure you it was me. Younger perhaps. The photograph is some years old.

> *(Silence.)*

I, ah … there might be a mix-up. Lucy, the woman in grey, seems to be alone.

CHARLES: I already asked her. Lou Sykes sent for her. He got cabin fever during the cold spell last month and ran off to the States.

CHARLOTTE: Oh.

CHARLES: She has to go back. Is there anyone from the Agency with you?

CHARLOTTE: No, not with us. They …why?

CHARLES: Somebody'd better tell her.

CHARLOTTE: Oh, ah, I think maybe … I don't know.

> *(Silence. CHARLES looks at the other women.)*

The rest of the women have someone meeting them. I believe you are here to meet me, Mr. Teeter.

CHARLES: Yeah. *(Silence.)* Uh, call me …

CHARLOTTE: Charles.

CHARLES: Yeah. Well. *(Silence.)* It is you.

> *(Silence.)*

CHARLOTTE: I never received your photograph. The Agency said the mails aren't reliable out here.

CHARLES: The photographer … was late comin'. The picture didn't turn out.

> *(Silence.)*

CHARLOTTE: My.

CHARLES: Eh?

CHARLOTTE: It's cold.

CHARLES: Yeah?

CHARLOTTE: It wasn't this cold back East. Not when we left four days ago.

CHARLES: It gets colder. Least last winter it did. This is my second one here. First winter the snow was five feet deep. Shared a tent with two Ukerainians.

CHARLOTTE: A tent!?

CHARLES: I got a sod hut built real quick last spring.

CHARLOTTE: Ah … you—

CHARLES: I'm not sharing with anyone now.

CHARLOTTE: Your application form said you owned a house!

CHARLES: Good as anyone else's for twenty miles. Or at least into town. Quarter section. All broken.

CHARLOTTE: Brok—? Where is the … your place?

CHARLES: Can just about see it from here. I'm east. North of the correction line three miles.

> *(The train has steam up for departure. Two short whistle blasts, bells ring. CHARLES and the CONDUCTOR overlap.)*

CONDUCTOR: *(Overlap.)* Booard! All aboard!! Train now leaving for Nestor, Ogilvy, Penstock, Quinquaid, and all points West. Board!

CHARLES: *(Overlap.)* It's productive land. I'm a good farmer.

> *(The whistle. The bell.)*

CHARLOTTE: This train, it …! Where is it going?

CHARLES: Out to the coast. Takes three days.

CHARLOTTE: And going back East?

CHARLES: Next week. Takes the same four days goin' back. That it for your bags?

CHARLOTTE: My trunk hasn't been shipped yet.

CHARLES: We have to be there pretty quick, let's go.

CHARLOTTE: We're going out to your property?

CHARLES: The hotel. The judge could only ride in today so all of us who ordered away for a bride got together and set up a group ceremony. Do all twelve at once.

CHARLOTTE: I—We just arrived!

CHARLES: Well, eleven now.

CHARLOTTE:—sitting on a train four days—

CHARLES: Hope you don't mind sayin' vows in front of a Justice of the Peace.

CHARLOTTE: My dress is in my trunk!

CHARLES: It'll all be legal, don't worry. Let's go. We're gettin' married.

> *(CHARLES takes her suitcase and leaves. Shrill whistle screech! The train pulls out, travels across prairie and disappears.)*

CHARLOTTE: *(The coat.)* I'll be keeping this.

*(RUSSELL storms up from the barn. CHARLOTTE enters the house. Winter changes to spring.)*

RUSSELL: Where the hell is this?!

EVA: Russell! This man told me the most—

RUSSELL: Just a second.

EVA: He knew your—

RUSSELL: In a minute! Well?! Massey Harris, Model Number—

HAROLD: That's Red. Good little tractor for plowin' gardens, shovelin' snow. Needs new brakes.

RUSSELL: Where is it?!

HAROLD: Over at the English place.

RUSSELL: Where is this guy?! The auction's tomorrow!

HAROLD: This guy's right here 'n he's bringin' it back in the mornin'. Name's Harold. Good to meet y', Russ.

RUSSELL: Russell. It belongs here.

HAROLD: I had a deal with yer Gran'. She'd let me borrow stuff if I kept this place goin'.

RUSSELL: … make sure it's back.

HAROLD: I said I would. 'Course, if I had'na kept the place up, you wouldn't have to be goin' through those lists today.

RUSSELL: What's that supposed to mean?

HAROLD: I dunno. I just said it, I don't have to know what it means.

*(RUSSELL makes notes on lists.)*

EVA: All this? You must work very hard to keep up.

HAROLD: This place ain't that big any more. Machines do the hard stuff. Thanks to guys like yer dad.

RUSSELL: Honey, time to get started.

EVA: Russell, this man knew your—

RUSSELL: It's almost noon, we haven't got all day.

*(Music.)*

HAROLD: I knew yer mother, too.

RUSSELL: Where's the nearest phone?

HAROLD: Down the hill at my place.

EVA: Russell …

*(RACHEL walks up the hill from the fields, wears overalls. A teenager. Sweaty and tired from work. RUSSELL and EVA don't see her.)*

RUSSELL: How far is it?

HAROLD: Walk it in ten minutes. That car'll prob'ly get 'y there before y' leave.

EVA: We were going to talk about this.

RACHEL: Time to stop daydreaming Harold.

RUSSELL: Is someone there?

HAROLD: Door's open.

RACHEL: Time for work.

EVA: Russell!

RUSSELL: You've had three days.

EVA: In that car? While you broke every speed limit in the country?

RACHEL: It's been a busy morning without you.

HAROLD: Y' haveta phone the Lawyer, too. There's a release t' say yer just as good as yer mother.

RACHEL: And now it's over.

RUSSELL: What's the number?

HAROLD: In the envelope.

*(RUSSELL goes back for the envelope. EVA sees RACHEL.)*

Eva says yer mom's …?

EVA: … in the Belgian Congo.

RACHEL: Go.

HAROLD: She used to be a real farm girl.

RACHEL: They need someone to run the steamer.

EVA: Not her.

RACHEL: If she thinks I will run that machine again she can kiss my ass.

HAROLD: Rachel.

EVA: That's her.

RACHEL: I didn't say anything. She wouldn't understand.

*(RACHEL goes into the house.)*

EVA: There isn't another woman senior to her in the whole Federal Government.

HAROLD: I've seen her plow behind a horse. Shovel fertilizer.

EVA: I can't believe we're talking about the same—

HAROLD: That's her. In fact he's standin' on the exact same spot where he was conceived.

> *(Silence.)*

Well, almost the exact spot. From as far as you guys came, it's close enough. It really happened in the barn, but right there's where yer folks first met.

RUSSELL: You don't know wh—

HAROLD: Fall 'a '24. I saw it.

RUSSELL: It's none of your business! Excuse us, we've got a very busy day.

EVA: She has never—

RUSSELL: There is a house full of stuff in there!

EVA: I thought you were going to make a phone call.

HAROLD: I'd just gone down to take over runnin' the steamer an' come right back up with a sprained wrist. A buggy drives in the yard. Top up, windows all done up. Steam on 'em it was so hot inside.

> *(ART runs to the shelter of the porch. Shields himself from the view. RACHEL appears behind the screen door.)*

ART: *(Croaks.)* Good day, Ma'am. Is the, ah, is the Farm Owner in this afternoon?

> *(Silence.)*

Hello? Excuse me, could you tell me if … is there anybody—?

RACHEL: It's harvest.

ART: … ah, yeah. A pretty good one I guess.

RACHEL: No one's home anywhere.

ART: … oh …

RACHEL: They're out stuffing themselves.

ART: … I see…. Could you tell your husband—

RACHEL: My father.

ART: Well, tell your father I called. My card.

> *(ART tries to hand the card to RACHEL. She doesn't open the door.)*

I'd like to sell him some machinery. Gas powered tractors. They're the way to go in farming these—

RACHEL: Talk to my father.

ART: Well. *(Finds a crack in the door, leaves the card.)* Make sure he gets this. I'll be staying at the Royal.

*(Silence.)*

… ah. Thanks. G'day.

*(ART can't step out from under the porch roof.)*

*(Croak.)* Have you got a—I need some water. Can I please have a drink?

RACHEL: The well's beside the barn.

ART: I can't g—! I have to have a drink!

*(Silence. She turns away. RACHEL disappears into the house. ART is trapped.)*

Just please can I—where'd you say—?

*(Footsteps. RACHEL gives ART a teacup of water.)*

Thanks. Thanks a lot. That was, ah, I really needed …

*(Silence.)*

Pretty hot … for September…. Is it alw—?

RACHEL: It's as hot as it is.

ART: Well, yeah, I guess. It's just that it isn't what I'm used to. Back East.

RACHEL: Where?

ART: Back East?

RACHEL: Yeah.

ART: Oh, everywhere. My address is my suitcase.

RACHEL: Have you been to the Palace Hotel?

ART: …? Yeah, sure.

RACHEL: I used to listen to music on the radio.

ART: The Starlighters?

RACHEL: I don't have a radio anymore.

ART: Everybody's got to have a radio.

RACHEL: My father disagrees.

ART: Radio's the thing of the future. You know how many people you could sell to if y—?

RACHEL: Do you like it here?

ART: Can't sell too many tractors to office people back home. I travel a lot. When you're good you have to. Head Office keeps me moving.

RACHEL: Back East?

ART: I'm going back end of the week for a special award banquet. Promotion. Divisional Sales Manager. Big salary.

RACHEL: Do you like it here?

ART: Huh? Out here? It, ah, isn't what I'd … it's where the sales are.

RACHEL: Do you like it?

ART: I'm so busy, I've got no time to, you know, worry about …

    *(Silence.)*

  This is a awful place.

    *(Silence.)*

  I don't know anyone out here. I don't get many chances to meet people.

RACHEL: You move around a lot.

ART: I leave in three days.

    *(Silence.)*

  What are you doing this afternoon?

RACHEL: I'm busy.

ART: I thought you might like to go for a ride.

    *(Silence.)*

RACHEL: I'm busy.

    *(RACHEL disappears into the house.)*

ART: Don't—! At least let me …! Hey?! … Thanks for the drink.

    *(ART heads across the yard. The screen door slams. RACHEL stands on the porch.)*

RACHEL: My parents are having a Harvest Party tonight.

ART:—huh …?

RACHEL: The whole District will be here.

ART: That's nice.

RACHEL: They're farmers. They buy tractors.

ART: Oh. I see. This'd be a pretty good place to be then. That's a good idea. I suppose I'd need an invitation.

RACHEL: Whoever wants to come here can.

ART: Maybe we can have a dance?

RACHEL: Not with a stranger.

    *(RACHEL reads ART's business card.)*

  My name is Rachel Teeter, Mr. Arthur Milligan.

*(The screen door slams. RACHEL disappears in the house. ART
runs to his buggy. Hot autumn to warm spring.)*

RUSSELL: Why are you here?!

HAROLD: Tidyin' things up for the auction.

RUSSELL: You're not helping. You don't own this place. Why don't
you take a break and go home.

EVA: You see, we only know her as she is today. The person you
describe is, ah, someone else, really.

HAROLD: That's what happened.

RUSSELL: I don't care what … bizarre fantasies you've concocted
over the last thirty—

HAROLD: I guess it ain't easy to think of yer mum gettin' excited
over a perfect stranger.

RUSSELL: That's it!

EVA: Russell! He's just—

RUSSELL: No one talks about her that way!

HAROLD: I'm sorry—

RUSSELL: You'd better be!

HAROLD:—you can't take the truth.

RUSSELL: I beg your pardon?!

EVA: Harold!

HAROLD: I said I'm sorry.

EVA: He said he's sorry.

RUSSELL: You've got it wrong.

HAROLD: That's the way it looked to everyone out here. She was
starvin' and he was a feast.

EVA: Harold! The woman we know is completely different.

HAROLD: Y' figure she couldn't get that—?

RUSSELL: Listen old man! You don't know what you're—!

HAROLD: I've been around.

RUSSELL: Around the barn.

HAROLD: More places 'n you have.

RUSSELL: Air Force. The Second War and Korea.

HAROLD: Merchant Marine. '28 t' '35. Around the world three times.

RUSSELL: I've flown it. Five confirmed kills in Korea, sixteen in the
Big One.

HAROLD: Average 30 bushels to the acre, 1939 to 1945.

    *(Silence.)*

RUSSELL: Get moving on the house.

EVA: It's not even noon yet.

RUSSELL: We haven't got all day!

HAROLD: Yer a lot like yer mother.

    *(RACHEL comes out of the house with a large square of cloth, rips strips, and bandages HAROLD's wrist.)*

RACHEL: Pretty stupid Harold.

HAROLD: Thought I could push the belt back on without stoppin'.

RACHEL: Throw you ten feet.

HAROLD: I hit your father.

RACHEL: Then he threw you ten feet.

HAROLD: No he stopped me fr—

RACHEL: So now he has to run the steamer? Well, that's not efficient is it?

HAROLD: He didn't seem—

RACHEL: He must have torn a strip off you. Stopping work. Not pulling together.

HAROLD: Well he couldn't really stop all the—

RACHEL: So close to the finish. Everybody's got to work their hardest.

HAROLD: Yer mum looked at it.

RACHEL: Some more than others.

HAROLD: They're almost finished. They, ah … I think they could slow down. *(Silence.)* I don't know where yer dad's gonna put it all. *(Silence.)* I heard yer mum got mad again. You walked away.

    *(Silence.)*

What're y' gonna do the resta the day?

RACHEL: Clean house.

HAROLD: For the party. I, ah, I was gonna ask y' to go?

RACHEL: I'm already here.

    *(Silence.)*

HAROLD: Who was that?

RACHEL: Who?

HAROLD: He just left.

RACHEL: Sells tractors.

HAROLD: Where's he from?

RACHEL: The city.

HAROLD: Back East?

RACHEL: I guess.

HAROLD: Where?

RACHEL: Somewhere not here.

> *(Silence.)*

HAROLD: You know, that time we climbed up on the barn roo—

RACHEL: Don't.

HAROLD: You 'n' me 'n' yer brother. We could see for fifteen mil—

RACHEL: You can't see a thing.

HAROLD: I know what I'm lookin' at.

RACHEL: But you can't see.

HAROLD: What else is there?

> *(Silence.)*

RACHEL: Next year. My brother. Something … anything that'll make a difference. *(Silence.)* Nothing. Count on not counting.

HAROLD: Lookit the crop this year, y'c'n count on that.

RACHEL: How do you feel today, Harold?

HAROLD: … kinda—well, 'cept fer this …

RACHEL: I feel great. Count on it. *(Silence.)* If it isn't grasshoppers, it'll be rust. If it isn't rust, it'll be prices. If it isn't prices, it'll be me. *(Silence.)* You won't be dancing with that arm.

> *(Screen door slam. RACHEL disppears in the house. Fall turns to spring.)*

RUSSELL: Wait until she hears this.

HAROLD: She wouldn't remember me.

RUSSELL: Because she doesn't waste her time living in the past. Like you, whining over a lost sweetheart.

HAROLD: T' get good at somethin', y' gotta practice.

RUSSELL: Wasted your life because you had a crush on my mother.

HAROLD: Growing' up together and all, everybody in the District thought we were gonna get married. I thought so too.

EVA: I think I'll get a start in the house.

HAROLD: I coulda been yer father.

EVA: Is it open? How do I, ah …?

HAROLD: Here. *(Tosses EVA the key.)* So y' understand it's curious t' hear y' were comin'. Wonderin' what y'd be like.

RUSSELL: Shut up old man.

HAROLD: I ain't old.

RUSSELL: You're senile.

HAROLD: That's a matter a' opinion.

EVA: Could you help me with this door? It—

> *(Music begins behind the door. A country dance band.)*

HAROLD: Funny the way things happen. Losin' a chance like that 'cause a' someone drivin' into the yard outa nowhere one day.

RUSSELL: We've wasted the entire—

HAROLD: Y' think about things like that a lot but they always surprise you. When y' hear about another one, I mean. They happen all the time.

RUSSELL: Just … stop talking about him!

HAROLD: Take yer Gran', fer instance. Hour 'n' half after she gets here, she's married to a stranger. For better 'r worse.

RUSSELL: I have to make a phone call.

HAROLD: Just down the hill. I'll tell Eva here about how you almost weren't born.

> *(CHARLES slams out of the house. RUSSELL doesn't leave.)*

So there's eleven couples partyin' on their wedding night. All crammed into the old Empress Hotel. It's burnt down now, but it wasn't too big.

> *(A small knock on the door.)*

CHARLES: Bugger off Cy!

HAROLD: The whole District's there, Elmer Huffman's sawin' away, everybody's dancin' up a storm.

> *(Another knock. CHARLES charges the door and opens it.)*

CHARLES: One more crack outa ya an' I swear I'm gonna—!

> *(CHARLOTTE stands in the doorway with two glasses of punch.)*

CHARLOTTE: Hello. I lost track of you again.

CHARLES: … been sittin' right here.

CHARLOTTE: The last time I saw you you were over by the punch bowl. Discussing freight costs.

CHARLES: Yeah. Discussin'.

CHRLOTTE: They seem like fine men.

CHARLES: They're all a bunch of fence posts.

CHARLOTTE: Oh ... perhaps it's too early to tell.

CHARLES: Take my word, they 're all gonna go under one by one.

CHARLOTTE: They seemed to feel strongly about your opinion.

CHARLES: It's the Truth is what it is. Ain't no opinions about Truth.

CHARLOTTE: Is that why you threw a cup of punch in his face?

CHARLES: He was askin' for it!

CHARLOTTE: So you obliged him?

> *(Silence.)*

I'm sorry. It's the school teacher in me.

> *(Silence.)*

So. You left the party and came out here?

CHARLES: I don't like to party with fence posts!

> *(Silence.)*

I, ah, don't mean to make it sound ... uh ... here, sit down.

CHARLOTTE: Well, it takes a while to make friends. *(Silence.)* Do you ever miss your home, Charles?

CHARLES: I live here.

CHARLOTTE: I mean, where are you from?

CHARLES: Back East. Country boy though. Don't come from a factory town.

CHARLOTTE: Oh. *(Silence.)* So that makes us different?

CHARLES: I didn't say—No. No, it don't. Well, maybe.

CHARLOTTE: *(Smiling.)* Probably a little.

CHARLES: My dad always used to say it takes all kinds. *(He smiles.)* An' he was sure one of 'em.

CHARLOTTE: *(Smiling.)* What was he like?

CHARLES: Dad? Crazy as hell. 'Scuse me. He's still kickin'. He can grow anythin'. I'll never be as good a farmer. Hope I never get as far behind. Great yields. Low prices.

CHARLOTTE: That's not his fault.

CHARLES: Well ... yeah. It is. It's everyone's fault if they don't make it their fault.

CHARLOTTE: Why did you leave?

CHARLES: Told ya, he could grow anythin'. Grew too many kids.

*(Silence.)*

CHARLOTTE: You're from a big family.

CHARLES: Only way to be.

CHARLOTTE: How many?

CHARLES: Twelve that lived. But on a place that size the eighth son don't get an inheritance. 'Cept knowin' farmin'. 'N' I got that in me. Farmin' and big families.

*(Silence.)*

CHARLOTTE: All those people dancing. I haven't yet but I have to catch my breath…. Thank you for having this party for us.

CHARLES: Huh? Oh, that ain't…. Somebody woulda come up with the idea.

CHARLOTTE: It helps us get to know people here. Get everybody dancing.

*(Silence. A polka has everyone up and flying. CHARLOTTE looks at CHARLES.)*

CHARLES: What're you starin' at?

CHARLOTTE: He's a good musician.

CHARLES: Elmer? Be a better farmer if he spent less time playin'.

CHARLOTTE: It's a lovely tune.

CHARLES: Look … I don't dance. Never any good at it.

CHARLOTTE: Have you ever tried?

CHARLES: Well, I … no, but—

CHARLOTTE: All those people dancing on their wedding night. No one will notice if you don't know the steps. It's almost over Charles.

*(Silence.)*

Come. Let's try.

CHARLES: … I can't do this.

CHARLOTTE: You've done harder things than this, I'm sure. I'll teach you the steps. It's a heel and toe polka. Just step once—

CHARLES: I got two left feet.

CHARLOTTE: In a room full of fence posts, two left feet are ahead of the game. It's easy if you try. Stand on your left foot. That's right. The left. Now, bounce once on the right heel, once on the toe. Then step off on the right for …

*(The polka ends. Cheers and applause from the dancers.)*

CHARLES: That's too bad, eh? I was just gettin' the …

ELMER (HAROLD): Last dance. Ev'body. Last dance.

> *(A slow country waltz.)*

CHARLES: … hang of it …

> *(The night begins to waltz around them.)*

CHARLOTTE: Shall we?

CHARLES: … I don't waltz.

CHARLOTTE: We won't do too badly if we try.

> *(Silence.)*

CHARLES: How do you start one of these deals?

CHARLOTTE: Hold my hand. The other on my waist.

> *(CHARLES holds CHARLOTTE in his arms for the first time. CHARLOTTE is held in CHARLES' arms for the first time.)*

Three steps to the right. Then three steps to the—all right, the left first.

CHARLES: And you'll keep out of the way?

CHARLOTTE: Oh yes.

> *(They begin waltzing.)*

That's fine. Just fine.

> *(They spin and turn to a delicate, old-timey country waltz.)*

There.

CHARLES: Yeah. Well … not bad.

CHARLOTTE: Not bad.

> *(CHARLES stops looking at his feet and into her eyes. They are dancing.)*

CHARLES: Yer pretty good at this.

CHARLOTTE: We'll get better if we practice.

CHARLES: Yeah?

> *(A small trip.)*

Sorry about that.

CHARLOTTE: Doesn't hurt.

CHARLES: Guess yer gonna have to be the one t' teach our kids to dance.

> *(CHARLOTTE stops. The waltz continues around them.)*

What's the matter? Did I hurt you?

CHARLOTTE: I … Charles—I'm older than you.

CHARLES: Yer application said—By how much?

CHARLOTTE: I'm over thirty.

CHARLES: How over?

CHARLOTTE: Thirty-eight.

CHARLES: Thirty-eight!! That, well, you don't look that bad.

CHARLOTTE: Thank you.

CHARLES: Why didn't you tell—

CHARLOTTE: Charles. I may not be able to have children.

> *(The waltz ends.)*

ELMER: Is it for tonight. No more. No. No. All played out. See you next time.

CHARLES: You never told me that.

> *(People wish them goodnight.)*

> *(Overlapping.)* Luke. 'Night Bill. Yeah. Tomorrow afternoon. Alec. Cy.

CHARLOTTE: *(Overlapping.)* Goodnight Annie. You too, … Ellie. Marie-Claire. I'll be in touch.

> *(Silence. The hall is empty.)*

CHARLES: Can't stay here. Getcher stuff.

CHARLOTTE: Charles, I—

CHARLES: You better come home with me for tonight.

CHARLOTTE: Is it a long way?

CHARLES: To my place? Not far for out here.

CHARLOTTE: Yes. To your place.

> *(A cold wind.)*

RUSSELL: She shouldn't have lied to him.

EVA: She was in love with him.

> *(CHARLES walks into winter night.)*

RUSSELL: She didn't even know him.

EVA: She told him.

> *(CHARLOTTE follows CHARLES.)*

RUSSELL: After they were married. She couldn't make it so she took the first guy that came along. Look at him.

EVA: He danced!

> *(Winter is now spring.)*

RUSSELL: And the wife he picks can't even hold up her end.

HAROLD: I dunno what I'd say if I found out there was a good chance I wouldna been born.

RUSSELL: But I was.

HAROLD: Odds were against it.

RUSSELL: Near misses don't exist. What's up ahead is the bear that'll bite.

HAROLD: Then y' gotta talk to that bear.

RUSSELL: The bear's the bear, bud. He don't talk. Let's get moving.

EVA: Pardon?

RUSSELL: The house. The list. It's past noon.

EVA: I'm hungry.

RUSSELL: You're always hungry.

EVA: Are there any places to eat around here?

HAROLD: Fong's in town or Rita's out on the highway.

RUSSELL: Later, babe. You've got a job to do.

EVA: We had breakfast at five-thirty! I'm getting a little—

RUSSELL: The house.

EVA: Russell!?

RUSSELL: Hey, if you're going to waste time listening to this guy? I've got most of this list done.

EVA: This is my holiday!

RUSSELL: Business, honey.

EVA: I'm going to help Harold.

HAROLD: That'd be nice.

RUSSELL: Look! If we are going to get this thing organized—

EVA: Harold is going to teach me about planting flowers.

    *(Silence.)*

RUSSELL: That the machine shed?

HAROLD: Can't miss it. Careful, it'll be dark in there.

RUSSELL: I'm going to make that call soon.

    *(RUSSELL saunters down to the machine shed.)*

HAROLD: Tufted Loosestrife. "Lysimachia Thyrisi-flora." Weak stems, fall over if other plants don't help hold 'em up.

EVA: I could kill him!

HAROLD: *(Offers a bedding plant.)* Throw this.

EVA: No, it—

HAROLD: Y' look like y' want t' throw somethin'.

EVA: I can't throw that!

HAROLD: What can y' throw then?

EVA: I've had—! If he—! *(Aaargh!)* He is so … ig-norant!!

HAROLD: Y' can kick the house. It's bein' torn down in two days.

EVA: No. It's all right. I'm fine.

HAROLD: Y' sure?

EVA: I'm fine!

HAROLD: Then how 'bout givin' me a hand!

> *(Silence.)*

EVA: I'm sorry. What can I do?

> *(HAROLD hands EVA his thermos.)*

HAROLD: Start by pourin' yerself a cuppa coffee, 'n I'll show y' what I know about this stuff. Then y' can bring me up t'date on the Teeters.

EVA: You know so much already.

HAROLD: Never met Russ before. Or you.

EVA: There's nothing special about us. *(Sips, chokes.)* What is in this?

HAROLD: Lemme try. Jeeze, y' know, if moonshine wasn' illegal I'd say that's what was in here. Well, sun's over the yardarm.

> *(EVA pours more.)*

EVA: We'll share.

HAROLD: First thing y' get things ready. See this guy? He's doin' his best, but y' gotta help 'im. So y' set everything up just right before y' begin. Start by diggin' a hole.

EVA: In here.

HAROLD: Can't dig in the porch. Jus' fine. So. You 'n' Russ. Met'm in the war, eh?

EVA: How'd you know?

HAROLD: He said he was in the war. You been married long enough. Y' still got a bit of an accent.

EVA: It slips out.

HAROLD: I c'n tell, 'cause I don't have one.

> *(Silence.)*

EVA: I was at the High Commission in London during the Battle of Britain, secretary to Russell's Mother. She was … so … important. To think that I was working with her I was just in…. *(Silence.)* I was very lucky. Caught up in something so big.

HAROLD: I missed alla that. Got differed 'cause 'a the farm.

EVA: I met Russell at a Commission affair. The Blitz was roaring. When we came back upstairs, the staff opened the curtains in the dark ballroom, and we watched the city by the light of its own flames. Russell arrived late from night Ops. He had downed two fighters. He smelled of cordite and petrol and … burned brighter than the fires in the next street. I felt as silly as a moth. *(Silence.)* All around me people, friends were dying. It was … easy to give yourself in those days.

HAROLD: Careful how y' dig. Jus' put some back.

EVA: The War ended, we got married, and … Palestine. Dutch Indonesia. Korea. Wherever the Air Force sent him. I haven't been home since.

HAROLD: Y' lived in Tokyo?

> *(Silence.)*

EVA: Just outside.

HAROLD: I had a lotta good times there. I like Japan.

EVA: Good for you!

> *(Silence.)*

HAROLD: Okay.

EVA: Sorry. *(Silence.)* What were you doing in Japan?

HAROLD: Freighter shippin' coal in '32 and '34.

EVA: 1951 for us.

> *(Silence.)*

It's just that … things used to be, during the War, things used to be…. Everything was for the last time, and that made it the first time each time. There weren't many options. Now Russell is … still the same. Or he's changed. And I'm the one who has to…. *(Silence.)* Husbands take a lot of getting used to. *(Silence.)* What do you know about husbands?

HAROLD: My dad was one. *(Silence.)* Isn't that usually the deal?

EVA: Mostly. *(Silence.)* Paul isn't Russell's baby.

> *(Silence.)*

He knows. When Paul … Russell was posted to an American aircraft carrier for four months. I know that doesn't seem long, but … that's the way we live. And … I went to a party at the officer's mess. One of his old flight buddies was there. I wasn't drunk. *(Silence.)* I wish time could go backward.

HAROLD: How's the baby?

EVA: Fine. *(Smile.)* He's my Little Man.

HAROLD: 'N Russ?

EVA: Russell? Hah. He just about …! In the Air Force, and the jobs he's looking for, you have to have a wife and family. Well, he's got one. Picture perfect. It … he leaves me alone. *(Silence.)* Paul was born when Russell was in Japan on business—he'd quit the Air Force by then. He came back. I showed him Paul. He looked at him in his crib. Paul started crying. Just hungry. And Russell … he was like a little boy. He's fought so many battles. I'd never seen him like that.

HAROLD: You still love him. Maybe y' can't have him.

*(Music.)*

Russell's dad—

EVA: Shut up! I don't want to hear any more of your stories!

HAROLD: Why would I want to tell you a story?

EVA: It doesn't …! I don't …!

HAROLD: Russell's dad came to the Harvest Party. Only about nine hours after he first met Russell's mum.

*(Party music from the house. Night, harvest moon. HAROLD puts on his wrist wrap. ART runs up to the house, RACHEL runs to the door to meet him. ART goes into the party.)*

Everyone was in the house dancin' on the lush bins of a great year. 'Cept me.

RACHEL: I knew you'd be moping.

HAROLD: How's the party?

RACHEL: Why don't you go in and dance?

*(HAROLD holds up his sprained wrist.)*

RACHEL: Harold.

HAROLD: Nice night.

RACHEL: Go inside with my father. You're both in the same mood.

*(RACHEL goes into the house.)*

HAROLD: I left.

EVA: You gave up.

HAROLD: I took a walk. Not very far.

*(RACHEL and ART come out of the house. ART carries a mason jar full of punch.)*

ART: Do we have to …? I'd just as soon …

RACHEL: You want to stay in there?

ART: Yeah, eh? Boy, your father … he's a stubborn—What is in this?

RACHEL: You've only just met him.

ART: You too. And your mother. Geeze, your mother!

RACHEL: Welcome.

ART: I kept talkin' to him, you know, and him and all his friends were listening, but, you know, and they were real hospitable—must of given me about four of these.

RACHEL: They're thirsty men.

ART: You know, but, none of 'em. Not a single one. They all just, sorta sat there. None of 'em movin'. You know they're all smilin' and bein' nice, but they're just … diggin' at me. Smilin' an' little insults alla time.

RACHEL: I don't want to talk about them.

ART: Everybody's waiting for your dad to say if he's gonna buy one or not. An' all I'm gettin' is insults!

RACHEL: Mr. Milligan. We haven't—It's getting late.

ART: Well, your old man—!

RACHEL: I'll tell you all about him, later. We can have time later. You must … let's talk about something else.

ART: Huh? Oh, sure. Nice night.

RACHEL: Art! *(Silence.)* Are you really going to be what you promised?

ART: When did I promise?

RACHEL: About being Division Manager.

ART: Oh, well, someday, sure. Yeah.

RACHEL: You won't work out here will you?

ART: *(Silence.)* No.

*(RACHEL takes ART's hand and leads him to the barn.)*

What? No!

RACHEL: What's the matter?

ART: Ah, no. No, let's stay—

RACHEL: Just a—

ART: No!

*(Silence.)*

Look—

RACHEL: Don't be afraid of my father.

ART: I can't, I … I'm afraid of open spaces.

RACHEL: What?

ART: I didn't know until I stepped off the train. I've never seen the sky. Like this, I mean. It, I … feel like I'm going to fall off the earth.

*(RACHEL laughs.)*

It's not my fault!

RACHEL: I know.

ART: You don't have to laugh at me.

RACHEL: What else is there to do?

ART: …?! I don't know. It's not nice.

RACHEL: *(Prairie and sky.)* But it's there.

ART: I know that that's there. I wasn't talking about that, I was talking about you laughing at me.

RACHEL: Walk with me.

ART: I can't! I don't see how you can stand it out here.

*(RACHEL takes the jar of punch and drinks.)*

RACHEL: You too.

ART: I've had, uh, enou—

RACHEL: Drink deep. And don't be afraid of the night. There's nothing out there to worry about.

ART: It's not the … the sky's too big.

RACHEL: The skies are never empty, Mr. Milligan, but there's nothing to pin your fears to. You left worse things in that room. *(Silence.)* My father's looking out there for something.

ART: I don't care what he's looking for.

RACHEL: That's what he's afraid of.

ART: What's he looking for?

RACHEL: My brother. His son. And you can't look.

*(Silence.)*

Another drink for both of us Mr. Milligan.

*(RACHEL drinks. She kisses ART. He tastes moonshine on her lips. EVA holds HAROLD back.)*

EVA: Harold don't.

HAROLD: I gotta stop her!

EVA: No!

RACHEL: A lovely night for a walk.

HAROLD: I love her.

EVA: You have to let Russell be born! For me.

> *(HAROLD pushes toward RACHEL and ART.)*

What about her?! Let her go!

RACHEL: The loft is full of summer hay and smells sweet.

EVA: She doesn't love you.

> *(RACHEL takes ART to the barn. They bump into HAROLD in the yard. Silence.)*

RACHEL: It's a Harvest Party.

> *(RACHEL walks with ART past HAROLD. He doesn't stop them.)*

Celebrate the end of the Old Year. It'll never come back again.

> *(RACHEL and ART go down the hill to the barn.)*

ART: Who's that silly bugger?

> *(HAROLD and EVA stand in the middle of the yard in the middle of the night.)*

EVA: Harold.

HAROLD: What.

EVA: Thank you. I know you didn't do it for me, but I wa—

HAROLD: Y' feel sorry for me? Easy for you! You think it ain't gonna happen with you'n Russell?

> *(EVA stands alone in the centre where she's always been.)*

… look … I didn't …

> *(EVA hurries away.)*

Damn. Just get out. Let's all take a break.

> *(Work and house lights snap up. HAROLD leaves. End of Act One.)*

# Act Two

*(House lights, work lights on. HAROLD starts early.)*

HAROLD: While we're waitin'… I don't get enough of a chance to do this in the show. How d'y' like my flowers? Nice to have somethin' beautiful around, eh? Of course there's no flowers. They haven't grown yet. But y' gotta admit it's a good idea.

*(Lights go out one by one.)*

Halfa sec. Saline Shooting Star. "Dodecatheon Pauciflorum." Tough little guy. Grows around alkali patches in the ditches. They ain't much. Just little pink flowers. But livin' on an alkali bed every little bit counts.

*(Blackout.)*

I can take a hint. We'll just start in, eh? Not much choice.

*(A bright spring afternoon. EVA comes out of the house. Silence.)*

EVA: I feel like a grave robber.

HAROLD: Y'r not robbin'.

EVA: I know. It's just that … her underwear and everything, it's all there.

HAROLD: Afraid 'a stumblin' across a hidey hole full 'a embarassin' stuff?

EVA: I wouldn't want people poking around my belongings.

HAROLD: They gonna find somethin'?

EVA: No!

HAROLD: Everybody's got stuff like it.

EVA: But I wouldn't want someone digging into it.

HAROLD: D' 'y think she cares?

EVA: How did she feel about it when she was alive?

42

HAROLD: She didn' like it.

EVA: That's good enough for me.

HAROLD: So what 'r y' gonna do?

EVA: Leave it for Russell.

HAROLD: Good thinkin'.

> *(Silence.)*

EVA: She has some nice things.

HAROLD: The will says everythin's supposed to be sold. But. Y' c'd prob'ly help y'self to some stuff if y' want.

EVA: And put them in the car? Why did Grandma want everything sold?

HAROLD: She didn' know you guys. An', uh, she had a difference of opinion with Russell's mother.

EVA: The money has to go to the town?

HAROLD: 'At's what the lawyer says.

EVA: What for?

HAROLD: Prob'ly the hockey rink.

EVA: No, I mean why did the will say someone from the family had to be here even though no one is getting any of the estate?

> *(RUSSELL walks up the hill. He has fallen into the repair pit in the machine shed—a thick goop of old machine oil, grease, dirt. Silence.)*

The inventory's going well. Just how many oil barrels are there?

HAROLD: Have any trouble findin' the machine shed?

> *(EVA and HAROLD laugh at RUSSELL. RUSSELL goes into the house.)*

HAROLD: Hasn' he got a sense of humour?

EVA: It got shot off in the war. What happened?

HAROLD: Machinery y' can't fix without getting' underneath, y' dig a deep hole so y' can. Looks like he found it.

> *(RUSSELL comes out of the house. He uses tea towels to clean himself.)*

Must be twenty-five years a' gunk down there. It's hard t' see in the dark if yer wearing sunglasses.

RUSSELL: Thanks for the warning.

EVA: He told you to be careful.

HAROLD: Halfa sec', those're Mrs. Teeter's fancy tea-towels.

*(RUSSELL continues.)*

HAROLD: They cost her a lot 'a money!

EVA: Don't.

*(EVA takes the towel RUSSELL is using and picks up the rest.)*

You could have used something else.

RUSSELL: Thanks for helping.

EVA: Go get a change of clothes.

*(EVA goes into the house.)*

RUSSELL: There's an awful lot of the day gone by!

*(RUSSELL stomps down to the car. Silence. Long silence.)*

HAROLD: If we were on radio, they'd call this dead air. Where was I? Shootin' Stars. If y' put 'em in yer garden, y' don't haveta worry too much about 'em. In fact, if y'd put 'em with a buncha pansies that can't fight back, y'd call it a weed.

*(EVA comes out of the house with some rags.)*

EVA: There's boxes of stuff in her sewing room.

HAROLD: Her projects. She never had the knack for 'em.

EVA: Think she'll mind?

*(RUSSELL comes up the hill. Carries a small suitcase.)*

HAROLD: I'll ask next time I see her.

EVA: At least I checked first.

*(EVA throws RUSSELL parts of clothing. He hesitates.)*

Oh use them!

*(EVA goes into the house. Silence.)*

RUSSELL: None of your business!

HAROLD: …?

RUSSELL: She's like this all the time.

HAROLD: Maybe it's something she didn' eat f' lunch.

RUSSELL: I beg your pardon?

HAROLD: She's drinkin' on an empty stomach.

RUSSELL: Where'd she get something to drink!?

HAROLD: In my thermos.

RUSSELL: Just what the hell do you think—!

HAROLD: She needed a rest from makin' up that list.

RUSSELL: How far did she get?

HAROLD: She hasn' started.

RUSSELL: I told her to get moving!

HAROLD: That's why she needed a rest.

RUSSELL: Look old man! I've got a busy day and important things to get done before—!!

HAROLD: Geeze, can it, eh?! We heard it already. *(Pause.)* Sorry. I'm busy too.

RUSSELL: What are you doing here?!!

HAROLD: I'm plantin' this year's garden.

RUSSELL: What for?!

HAROLD: If y' don't plant, they won't come up.

RUSSELL: The house is being torn down in two days!!

HAROLD: I admit it's a long shot.

> *(Silence.)*

RUSSELL: You're nuts.

HAROLD: It helps.

> *(EVA comes out of the house. She wears a dress from another time. EVA throws a pair of overalls at RUSSELL.)*

RUSSELL: What's that?

EVA: Your grandfather's overalls.

RUSSELL: That.

EVA: Nice, isn't it?

RUSSELL: We have no time for fooli—?

EVA: You can't get material like this now.

RUSSELL: Take it off.

EVA: What do you think?

HAROLD: It suits you.

EVA: I think so.

RUSSELL: And you're finished?! Is that why you can goof off like this?!

EVA: There's no point doing the list until I decide what I want to take.

RUSSELL: Honey, be sensible.

EVA: Harold said he'd ship them.

HAROLD: I … did.

> *(Far-off sound of rain.)*

EVA: *(Overlap with RUSSELL.)* I love the dining room suite. Do you think the table comes apart? The china cabinet would be heaviest.

RUSSELL: *(Overlap with EVA.)* You know the size of those apartments!

> *(RUSSELL pulls EVA away. A soft drumming of rain.)*

What is it?! We have more work here than you can handle and no room to take anything! I am not going to haul old furniture around the world!

> *(A rainy afternoon. RACHEL climbs the hill. A middle-aged businesswoman.)*

EVA: I want something to remember them by.

RUSSELL: No!

RACHEL: … catch my breath …

> *(RUSSELL sees his mother. Silence.)*

… hello. It's steeper than I remember.

RUSSELL: Why is she—?

EVA: She came back! I remember she—during the War—she just dropped everything and flew out.

RACHEL: They got my telegram?

HAROLD: Yesterday.

RACHEL: Is Mother …?

HAROLD: She'll be out.

RACHEL: Father?

HAROLD: Gone inside.

> *(Silence.)*

RACHEL: I came from London with the dispatches, then a ride west with a training flight. A squadron of new bombers.

HAROLD: You're off fightin' the War now.

RACHEL: Well, not—I suppose.

> *(Silence.)*

It's been a while.

HAROLD: Coupla days anyway.

EVA: Harold.

HAROLD: Didn't think you'd notice. Bein' so important now.

EVA: Don't, please.

HAROLD: She's the one that snuck outa here!

RUSSELL: She had a right to.

RACHEL: Harold, I didn't—

HAROLD: Excuse me. I don't know diplomatic protocol for these occasions.

RACHEL: Harold—! I've just come from a lot of fighting and—

HAROLD: Any survivors? Who're we more worried for: the dead ones or the survivors?

EVA: *(Overlap with RACHEL.)* Harold!

RACHEL: *(Overlap with EVA.)* Please?

EVA: Just tell her!

> *(Silence.)*

RACHEL I wrote a speech during the flight. Sitting on sacks of mail. The letters home. Now it's … somewhere back over the Atlantic. *(Silence.)* I remember when he built this for her. This is like a dream now. It can't be real, but…. *(Silence.)* In London everything is so immediate. Air raid sirens. Bombers. Only two days ago. Funny what you can get used to. *(Silence.)* You look well.

HAROLD: I was Town Drunk for a coupla years. The bottom fell outa that 'cause 'a Prohibition. Then I went sailin'. Now I'm back. Doin' my bit for the War.

RACHEL: How's it goin', eh?

> *(Silence.)*

HAROLD: A few days were okay.

RACHEL: It's your memory. I have the opposite facility. I, ah … I'm glad you haven't changed. I left a few things here. Maybe you know where they are.

> *(Silence.)*

Dad used to tell us stories. Little pieces of nonsense: him standing in the fields, talking to a drought, or the wind, or early frost. Do you remember?

HAROLD: She was askin' me to remember. I'd been around the world three times rather than remember.

RACHEL: It's harder to forget than remember. But it works.

> *(Silence.)*

HAROLD: At night y' can hear for miles up here.

> *(Day narrows into a golden sunset.)*

Dog's barkin' in the next district. Trains pullin' out a' the elevator in Nestor. Y' sit out here, listen to it all go by. About then is when your dad used to come up from the fields.

*(CHARLES walks up the hill.)*

RACHEL: My brother and I would wait for him. Sometimes he'd be very late.

CHARLES: Hey, what's this? The two of y' been workin' hard all day?

RACHEL: We waited up for you.

CHARLES: Sleepy heads off to their beds.

RACHEL: Tell us a story first.

CHARLES: Morning gets here pretty quick thes—

RACHEL: Please?

CHARLES: Button, I'm tired.

RACHEL: We'll go right to bed after.

CHARLES: Promise?

*(RACHEL crosses her heart and spits to die.)*

Y'll probly fall back to sleep before I'm done. Okay, let's see. Once upon a time ... I think I've forgotten this one.

RACHEL: There was a man who grew wheat.

*(While CHARLES tells a story, CHARLOTTE stands in the house and listens. Her family never knows she is there.)*

CHARLES: And he worked all day and all night but he never got anywhere. Insects, diseases, all sortsa troubles, and pretty soon he was goin' broke. But he noticed some plants survived all that. He grew those seeds away from all the rest an' kept growin' 'em until they'd become a whole new plant that could take on all comers. He stored 'em for the winter, but the bin leaked and the grain rotted. He scrounged until he found a handful of good seeds and only seven of those germinated. He planted 'em, but his mule broke through the fence, started eatin' 'm. He stopped it just before it ate the last one. He saved that. He was back to seven seeds. An' he started again. Now we've all got his plants. With this, and time, y' got that. *(His land.)* Y' can feed everyone.

*(The children are asleep. CHARLOTTE disappears inside the house.)*

Told y' y'd fall asleep. Oogeeze. Stiffer 'n' Granma's corset. Where's yer mother? Help carry y' t' bed.

*(CHARLES goes into the house.)*

RACHEL: Strange. His stories. Not much of anything except ... he got up each morning. Faced all this.

HAROLD: Some days are tougher than others.

RACHEL: I have to talk to him Harold.

HAROLD: He wouldn't listen.

RACHEL: I'll take my chances.

>*(Silence.)*

HAROLD: Now how 'bout you tell me one about you.

RACHEL: ... you wouldn't be interested in what I've been doing.

HAROLD: It's a subject of continuin' fascination to me.

RACHEL: It's all too ... it's ... different now.

HAROLD: Then tell me about the night you left.

>*(Silence.)*

RACHEL: It's ... been a long time.

HAROLD: You forgot?

RACHEL: No I haven't forg—

HAROLD: Then tell me abo—

RACHEL: I haven't much time, I have to—! You think I haven't thought about that night? You think I haven't tried to find a way to ...?!

>*(Silence.)*

I remember a washtub full of punch. A hot night. A fog of hay dust ... the stars. The night out there.

>*(Spring afternoon to autumn night and a harvest moon.)*

HAROLD: The band playin' a schottische. Dancers rattlin' the borrowed china. Yer Dad holdin' court. Bein' out in the barn, you don't remember this part. I had five jars a' punch. I thought that was pretty good fer a first timer.

>*(CHARLOTTE hurries out of the house. She sees HAROLD. She collects herself.)*

CHARLOTTE:—! ... hello ...

>*(HAROLD vomits.)*

CHARLOTTE: What is ...?! Harold?! Don't ... just ... will you be—are you all right?

HAROLD: ... oh ... yer nasturtiums ...

CHARLOTTE: Do you ... need anything?

HAROLD: ... no, that's most of it ... things catch up on y', I'm sorry, geeze I'm stupid ... I gotta sit down ...

CHARLOTTE: I'll get your parents to drive you home.

HAROLD: No. No. Don't. I'm, he'd about give me—... jes, I'm, lemme ... I feel better, honest.

CHARLOTTE: Where's Rachel?

HAROLD: ...!

CHARLOTTE: Things have to be cleaned up for supper.

HAROLD: The party t' end all parties, eh?

CHARLOTTE: After all these years, it's expected.

HAROLD: 'Specially with how well everythin's goin'.

CHARLOTTE: ... of course ...

HAROLD: Y'should be havin' fun.

CHARLOTTE: People have to be taken care of.

HAROLD: 't's hard work.

CHARLOTTE: Parties? No.

HAROLD: I mean, all this. *(The farm.)*

> *(Silence.)*

CHARLOTTE: This is easy. It's all there. Even if it goes wrong. It's still there, you can touch it. *(Silence.)* Unlike some things.

> *(The party slides into a twisted distance.)*

HAROLD: Did you get that one?

RACHEL: Yes.

HAROLD: It's your brother she was talkin'—

RACHEL: I know! *(Silence.)* Twenty years. *(Silence.)* She's going to come out that door and—again—I'm going to be the first born. Who lived to see her brother die.

HAROLD: If he woulda lived he woulda been your uncle. Spanish Flu, 1918, went through here in a big way. Mrs. Teeter was pinnin' all her hopes on Rachel's brother. The flu didn't touch anybody but him.

> *(Music slips into another time.)*

RACHEL: That day, she sat there. Watching Dad walk around the old property line.

> *(RACHEL is either young or old.)*

Mother?

CHARLOTTE: Hush!

RACHEL: You want me to see if Mr. English's gone to town for the doctor?

CHARLOTTE: He's been spared the trouble.

> *(Silence.)*

RACHEL: Can I do som—?

CHARLOTTE: Time for chores.

> *(CHARLES walks up the hill. He carries four large, rusty metal stakes.)*

You have your brother's, too.

> *(RACHEL turns on HAROLD.)*

RACHEL: That's how it was! It's that ... small. From then on.... *(Silence.)* I can't even remember what it was like before that any more.

HAROLD: Nobody can.

CHARLOTTE: Child?!!

> *(RACHEL runs down the hill to the barn. Silence.)*

And now I just tell you?

CHARLES: A dozen years ago, me and the Krysa brothers walked from town along two wagon ruts that stopped just past their place. Thought I was lost. Found this surveyor's stake, an' then the others. I thought I wasn't lost any more.

> *(CHARLES drops the stakes. A harsh loud clang of metal. CHARLES goes into the house alone. Autumn night returns. A loud burst of music and dancing from the Harvest Party. Silence.)*

CHARLOTTE: *(The farm, the party.)* This ... isn't enough.

> *(ART stumbles up the hill from the barn.)*

ART:—! Hi. Uh. G'night.

> *(ART heads down to his wagon.)*

CHARLOTTE: Your hat Mr. Milligan. I'll get it for you.

> *(CHARLOTTE goes into the house.)*

EVA: Why didn't she—? Didn't she know?

HAROLD: You can see about fifty square miles from up here.

ART: Really.

HAROLD: There's only two thousand of us in the District.

ART: I'm just—

HAROLD: That makes us a pretty small neighborhood.

ART: Tell her I'll buy ano—

HAROLD: That's kinda contrary to what y'd think, don't you think?

> *(CHARLES and CHARLOTTE come out of the house.)*

CHARLES: You're goin' are y'?

> *(Silence.)*

ART: If you'll excuse me?

CHARLES: You're not gettin' away that easy.

ART:—?!!

CHARLES: Y' think y' can just waltz outta here?

> *(RACHEL comes out of the house. She eats a piece of cake.)*

ART: … gee, I gotta—

CHARLES: We haveta talk tractors.

ART: I'm sorry but, ah, I have—oh?

CHARLES: Got a coupla other guys thinkin' about it too.

ART: Ah, well, you know, really it's getting—

HAROLD: … uh, Mr. Teeter—

RACHEL: Please stay, Mr. Milligan.

CHARLOTTE: Put that back. It's for the guests.

HAROLD: Look, I don't know how t'—

RACHEL: I thought it hospitable to invite Mr. Milligan to stay.

HAROLD: There's somethin' y' should know!

> *(RACHEL walks to HAROLD.)*

RACHEL: I was talking with him about tractors. Quite modern. Everyone's going to look into them sooner or later.

> *(RACHEL casually takes HAROLD's arm. The sprained one.)*

Sorry. *(Silence.)* Who knows? Maybe one day they'll invent a machine so Harold won't get hurt during harvest. Will you stay, Mr. Milligan?

> *(Silence.)*

ART: I, ah…. How about I come back tomorrow? Happy to do business then. Besides, parties are for having a good time.

CHARLES: Make it after supper. Me and the Miss's'll be out 'til then.

RACHEL: I'll be home all day. If they're late, someone will be here.

ART: Fine. Great. I'll be here. Goodnight. And thank you.

CHARLES: Don't worry 'bout gettin' to the hotel. The horse ain't nearly drunk as you.

CHARLOTTE: Goodbye Mr. Milligan.

CHARLES: G'day.

RACHEL: Say goodbye to our guest.

> *(Silence.)*

HAROLD: Bye.

ART: See you tomorrow.

> *(ART leaves. CHARLES goes into the party.)*

CHARLES: Good thing he doesn't have to be smart when he's sellin' somethin' like that.

CHARLOTTE: *(To RACHEL.)* Supper's late.

> *(CHARLOTTE goes into the house.)*

RACHEL: Yes Mother.

> *(The party fades into soft rain and a grey afternoon.)*

Why didn't you—?!! *(Silence.)* You could have stopped him! You could have shouted rape! All this would have—!

HAROLD: Everyone would have known about it.

RACHEL: So?! Everyone did anyway! He wouldn't have—

HAROLD: How's I supposed to know y' were gonna run away the next day?!

RACHEL: What would you have done if I hadn't?

> *(CHARLOTTE comes out of the house. Silence.)*

Hello.

> *(Silence.)*

How have you—?

CHARLOTTE: Will you get Charles, please?

> *(HAROLD goes into the house. Silence.)*

You waited too long.

RACHEL: Didn't we all?

CHARLOTTE: You haven't changed.

RACHEL: Mother—! I asked the driver to wait. I can't stay.

CHARLOTTE: You haven't changed.

RACHEL: I won't take much of your time. I came to talk to Father.

> *(HAROLD brings CHARLES out of the house.)*

CHARLOTTE: He would have been glad to know.

> *(CHARLOTTE and HAROLD seat CHARLES. Silence.)*

RACHEL: This isn't him.

HAROLD: He got taken away.

RACHEL: No. This isn't him.

HAROLD: 'At's him.

RACHEL: No. He's a v—! No, I remember—clear as yesterday. Remember the stories he used to tell? We'd be sitting on his lap?

CHARLOTTE: Harold.

HAROLD: Yes Mrs. Teeter.

CHARLOTTE: I think he's getting a chill.

RACHEL: No!

CHARLOTTE: Don't raise your voice in front of your father!

RACHEL: I came all the way from …! *(Silence.)* You see, the world out there, it … there are madmen … things I could never imagine. I mean, I can say that about being brought up here. Never in my worst days did I think like…. *(Silence.)* It's hard to know when you're doing right. We hear stories—every High Commision in London is drafty with rumours. And documentation. *(Silence.)* They have … farms to kill people. *(Silence.)* I need to hear his stories.

HAROLD: He ain't here. He had a stroke on a rainy day and almost died with his face in the mud.

RACHEL: No.

CHARLOTTE: His health stopped when you left.

RACHEL: Mother plea—

CHARLOTTE: Twenty years. Watching. Every day. You've come back.

RACHEL: I forgot something.

CHARLOTTE: There's nothing for you.

RACHEL: Mother, I didn't mean for this to—

CHARLOTTE: Your place was here!

RACHEL: Maybe! But not as what you wanted me to be.

CHARLOTTE: I promised him!

RACHEL: And what did you promise me?!

> *(Silence.)*

My brother died. After that … you never saw me.

CHARLOTTE: I saw what happened when you left.

RACHEL: I left because you—!

> *(Silence. RACHEL stands alone in the centre.)*

Which came first? *(Silence.)* I have to go, a conference, Iceland of all places, in two days. I, ah … I'll write a cheque, expenses and medication. Shall I …? I'll give it to the doctor.

*(RACHEL hugs CHARLES.)*

It hasn't changed.

HAROLD: I guess not.

*(RACHEL walks away from her mother and down the hill.)*

RUSSELL: Wonder why she never talks about this place?

EVA: But, Charlotte wouldn't …?

HAROLD: That's what happened.

EVA: … how could she?

HAROLD: She couldn't do anything else.

CHARLOTTE: Harold?

HAROLD: Right.

EVA: What happened to Charles?

CHARLOTTE: We must take him inside.

HAROLD: He disappeared in a coupla days.

*(CHARLOTTE and HAROLD lift CHARLES.)*

CHARLOTTE: Careful. His legs get tangled easily. Lift under … that's it, come with me. There. Now you're standing.

*(CHARLES stands with CHARLOTTE. She looks into dead eyes. Silence.)*

There's no one to say goodbye to.

*(HAROLD takes CHARLES through the door and into the house.)*

RUSSELL: She deserves it.

CHARLOTTE: Harold?!

RUSSELL: Oh spare me. Harold?!

*(HAROLD comes out of the house.)*

HAROLD: Yeah?

CHARLOTTE: *(Overlap with RUSSELL.)* Harold?

RUSSELL: *(Overlap with CHARLOTTE.)* Harold?

HAROLD: *(To RUSSELL.)* Ssshhh! *(To CHARLOTTE.)* Yeah?

CHARLOTTE: Did I get a letter?

HAROLD: Rachel wrote.

CHARLOTTE: And.

HAROLD: Y' got a great grandson.

*(CHARLOTTE looks at RUSSELL. Silence.)*

CHARLOTTE: They say the days get shorter as you get older.

*(CHARLOTTE leaves. The day returns to spring afternoon.)*

RUSSELL: I will have nothing that belonged to that woman in my house!

EVA: Why do you have to make it her fault?

RUSSELL: If she is going to treat my mother like that, I should have respect for her?

EVA: What time is it?

RUSSELL: Damn! Where'd you say the phone was?

HAROLD: The white house. In the kitchen.

RUSSELL: I'll be a little while.

HAROLD: Where y' phonin'?

RUSSELL: Tokyo. I'll pay for it.

HAROLD: I phoned here from there once. Sounded like I was talkin' ta buncha chickens.

*(RUSSELL heads to his car.)*

EVA: Russell?

RUSSELL: I'll be right back.

EVA: Russell! At least tell me.

RUSSELL: If you're going to get like this aga—

EVA: I'll get how I damn well please! Tell me what you're going to tell them.

*(RUSSELL heads to his car.)*

I don't want to go.

RUSSELL: You know what this job means.

EVA: It's not fair to Paul.

RUSSELL: We discussed this!

EVA: No!! Everything with you is just—*(Silence.)* I have to have a vote.

RUSSELL: Yeah? Well you've been known to vote on your own.

*(Silence.)*

I have to make a call.

EVA: Then it's over.

RUSSELL: I beg your pardon?

EVA: I should take this off.

RUSSELL: Come back here!

EVA: Don't you have a call to make?

> *(EVA goes into the house.)*

RUSSELL: You'll get some work done?!

> *(RUSSELL leaves. Collides with HAROLD.)*

Outta my way!!

> *(RUSSELL heads to his car.)*

HAROLD: Some people's kids! Hope he didn—*(Looks at the plant he carries.)* Still okay. 'Course it'd take a lot t' get rid a'.

> *(Down the hill, expensive imported car door slam. Expensive imported car not starting several times.)*

Poison Ivy. "Pain-In-The-Caboosus." Want t' see? No? Thought I'd put some in. It turns up whether y' want it or not, might as well figure it in at the start.

> *(Starter motor whine.)*

Y' could put in wild oats and quack grass too but you can only go so far.

> *(Starter motor whine.)*

Geeze, y'know I'd tell y' more, but who wants to hear about someone else's troubles?

> *(Starter motor whine.)*

He'll run out a' patience soon. Besides there's only seven of that sound on the tape.

> *(Expensive imported car door slam.)*

That musta taken off a coat a' paint.

> *(RUSSELL storms up the hill.)*

RUSSELL: Is there a service station in this place?

HAROLD: Westley's Full Service on the highway. Next t' Rita's.

> *(RUSSELL goes to the house.)*

RUSSELL: I have to phone for a tow.

HAROLD: It's down there.

RUSSELL: What is?!

HAROLD: That's where the pho—

RUSSELL: I knew that. Eva!

HAROLD: She's takin' a nap.

RUSSELL: E—va!

HAROLD: Don't!

RUSSELL: Shut up! Eva!!

HAROLD: You shut up!

>*(RUSSELL charges HAROLD.)*

RUSSELL: What??!!

HAROLD: It's not good for the flowers.

>*(RUSSELL knocks the plant out of HAROLD's hand.)*

That ain't much better.

RUSSELL: You don't belong here! Leave!

HAROLD: I'm plantin'. Minus the one you just—

RUSSELL: The house is being torn down in two days!

HAROLD: Y' want everythin' t' look nice for the auction t'morrow?

RUSSELL: These flowers aren't even blooming!!

HAROLD: That's not my fault!!

>*(Silence.)*

RUSSELL: You're insane.

HAROLD: So I've gathered.

RUSSELL: What gives you the—?! I don't even know you!

HAROLD: Y' never get t' pick y'r neighbors. Jus' think, y' coulda got someone worse.

>*(Silence. RUSSELL goes.)*

Y' sure y' want t' use my phone?

RUSSELL: Yes!

HAROLD: Great. Everyone's never heard anyone talkin' t' Tokyo.

RUSSELL: What!?

HAROLD: It's a party line. Fifteen places. Nearest single line's over at the switchboard in Leaver.

>*(RUSSELL destroys a flower pallet.)*

RUSSELL: God!—damn!—hicks!—god!—damn!—son!—of!—a!—bitch!—middle!—of!—no!—where! I-can't-do-business-on-a-party-line!!

HAROLD: Reminds me of a—

RUSSELL: Will you shut up with that!!

HAROLD: This is a joke, really.

RUSSELL: You think you've got so many troubles? Like you're something special because you lost your sweetheart?

HAROLD: I remember one time—

RUSSELL: That's it!! You figure you can sit up here and complain about your crappy life?! Singin' the blues like you've got a monopoly? You don't know nothing about what it's like out there!

HAROLD: How 'bout tellin' me one I haven' heard?

RUSSELL: You want to hear something?!

> *(Silence.)*

Huh?

HAROLD: Go ahead.

RUSSELL: How about watching your old man drink himself to death while he lets you and your mother starve? All before you're six years old. In the middle of the thirties. How about watching your mother go through that?

HAROLD: Yeah, we heard about that wh—

RUSSELL: That ain't nothin' like going through it! She couldn't even get a job!

HAROLD: And look where she is now.

RUSSELL: The bastard wouldn't even marry her!

> *(Silence.)*

HAROLD: I didn' know that. Then that means you're a—

RUSSELL: I know what I am! I grew up with it.

HAROLD: That means you're a Teeter. *(Pause.)* There was a night when I coulda done somethin' about that.

RUSSELL: Why didn't you?

> *(Silence.)*

HAROLD: I chickened out. I've had to grow up with that. *(Silence.)* If I hadda done somethin', you wouldna been born.

> *(Silence.)*

Can I offer y' a drink?

> *(HAROLD pours a lidfull for RUSSELL. Empties the thermos.)*

This's got a slug a' the good stuff in it.

> *(RUSSELL drains the cup.)*

… glad y' liked it. [The Assistant Stage Manager's name]?

RUSSELL: That's awful.

> *(The A.S.M. comes out on stage.)*

HAROLD: *(To A.S.M.)* Couldja fill this up again, please.

*(The A.S.M. takes the thermos and leaves.)*

Yeah. I prob'ly shouldna used instant coffee but it cuts the flavor of the alcohol an' y' don't have t' add water.

RUSSELL: Tastes like dirty antifreeze. More.

HAROLD: [A.S.M.]'ll be back in a sec'. Y'r prob'ly a conisoor a' fine hooch. Bein' in the wars 'n' all.

*(RUSSELL gives a small snort: "You ain't kidding.")*

Too bad yer not a pilot anymore.

RUSSELL: Who said that?

HAROLD: I figgered since y' were lookin' f' a job—

RUSSELL: I'm the best damn flyer this country's ever seen.

*(The A.S.M. brings back the full thermos.)*

HAROLD: Great, thanks.

*(The A.S.M. leaves. HAROLD re-fills the cup, offers it to RUSSELL. RUSSELL takes the thermos.)*

Okay. I've never flown.

RUSSELL: Scared.

HAROLD: Yup. *(Hooch wheeze.)* Smooth. So. What's t' miss in flying?

RUSSELL: If you have to ask, you'll never know.

HAROLD: Just like drivin' a car only there's no road, right?

RUSSELL: You ain't even near. Put about ten of your guys on the same road against twenty of theirs. Speed everything up until you can't think. Then make it cost a lot.

HAROLD: What d' y' mean?

RUSSELL: Get it right, you land. Get it wrong, you crash.

HAROLD: What? That'd be like killin' me if my crop don't come up?

RUSSELL: You'd get a better crop.

HAROLD: I got no control over the rain.

RUSSELL: If you're going to do it, do it right. There's no room for mistakes.

HAROLD: Y' mean like Eva? Her not wantin' t' go 'cause of the kid. I see your point. She's selfish, eh?

*(Silence.)*

RUSSELL: She'll calm down.

HAROLD: I hear those big corporations really like t' see a happy family man. Geeze, hold on! Y' think if she doesn't go they won't give y' the job?

*(Spring begins to narrow into winter night. Cold wind.)*

That'd be too bad, eh? Wouldn' it be great if y' could ditch her an' still get the job? That'd be perfect. Just crash 'er.

RUSSELL: Shut up.

HAROLD: That's the way it goes. Crash or land.

RUSSELL: Shut the hell up.

HAROLD: Rules are rules. What's up ahead is the bear that'll bite. Jus' think about how yer Gran'd a' done.

*(CHARLES enters, carrying a blanket. Creates a sleigh using a bench or the suitcase.)*

Thousandsa miles from anywhere, her first night in town, and the guy she married doesn' love her an' doesn' want t' marry her.

RUSSELL: She deserved what she got.

HAROLD: Don't we all?

*(CHARLOTTE enters. Sleigh bells and a horse neigh. CHAR-LOTTE sits beside CHARLES, wraps herself in the blanket. CHARLES gee's the horse and drives a snowy trail. Silence.)*

CHARLOTTE: … beautiful!

CHARLES: Huh?

CHARLOTTE: I've never seen such …

CHARLES: The Aurora. Northern Lights.

CHARLOTTE: They're so … mysterious.

CHARLES: They're out all the time.

CHARLOTTE: They're dancing. You can almost hear their music.

*(CHARLES looks at her. The sky.)*

Maybe I've got dancing on my mind.

*(Silence. Jingle of harness throughout.)*

It doesn't feel as cold as this afternoon.

CHARLES: Yer gettin' used to it.

CHARLOTTE: After ten hours, do you think? It's the cold they warned me about.

*(Silence.)*

This is a dream. The long train ride out here. Eleven couples married at the same time. The dance. This night. The … "Aurora Borealis." Now I'm here. Riding a sleigh in the middle …

CHARLES: You mean: "in the middle of nowhere"?

CHARLOTTE: I mean … this is all new to me, Charles.

CHARLES: There's nothin' here 'cause it hasn't been built yet. There's a chance to get it right the first time. Ho. Get up there.

*(Silence.)*

CHARLOTTE: A nice sleigh. And comfortable.

CHARLES: It's not mine. Borrowed it from Bill English.

CHARLOTTE: What's your horse's name?

CHARLES: Horse.

CHARLOTTE: Oh?

CHARLES: Just got her.

CHARLOTTE: How did you get around before?

CHARLES: Walked.

CHARLOTTE: Cold.

CHARLES: Your breath just freezes and hangs in front of your face.

CHARLOTTE: Now I am beginning to feel chilly.

CHARLES: But there's people to talk to in town. When I needed to talk.

CHARLOTTE: Yes. I found living alone gives a lot of time to form opinions.

*(Silence.)*

Thank you for dancing with me, Charles.

CHARLES: Huh?

CHARLOTTE: You learned so quickly. You dance very well. I mean, did you see, what was his name …? The short man?

CHARLES: Glasses, brown suit?

CHARLOTTE: That's him.

CHARLES: Ed Grunfeld.

CHARLOTTE: I've never seen anyone dance like that.

CHARLES: Station clerk for the C.P. *(Spits at the mention of the corporation.)*

CHARLOTTE: He was so nervous.

CHARLES: You noticed his toupée?

CHARLOTTE: *(Laughing.)* Besides that.

CHARLES: It's the bride they sent him.

CHARLOTTE: Marie-Claire is a wonderful girl. A little … brassy.

CHARLES: Tall, too. Ed says she isn't what he wrote away for on the application form.

CHARLOTTE: There's a dif—

CHARLES: He's going to sue the Agency.

> *(Silence.)*

CHARLOTTE: That's all they are? An application form?

CHARLES: That's all he had to go on.

CHARLOTTE: But after this afternoon—

CHARLES: A deal's a deal.

CHARLOTTE: There are things that won't fit on an application form.

CHARLES: Like you being older'n me?!!

> *(Silence.)*

CHARLOTTE: That's important to you.

CHARLES: Yer damn right!

CHARLOTTE: I never knew.

CHARLES: Y' shoulda told me ya couldn' have kids!

CHARLOTTE: I didn't say I couldn't. I said I might not be able to.

CHARLES: Well, that's somethin' isn' it? Huh? "Might not?" What the hell's the point of this whole thing anyway if ya can't have kids?!

CHARLOTTE: Did you look for someone just to—

CHARLES: You think I woulda picked a … a old maid if I hadda—!?

CHARLOTE: Spinster, Charles! We're called spinsters.

CHARLES: I don't care if yer called an old biddy! Yer goddamn near twice as old as me!!

CHARLOTTE: That bother you young man?

CHARLES: What!!

CHARLOTTE: This is how you run your property? Just call something worn out and throw it away? Is this the way you're going to treat your family?

CHARLES: I know I can at least have a family!

CHARLOTTE: A farmer who's sewn wild oats?

CHARLES: Huh? Well, uh ya … can't expect a man t'—

CHARLOTTE: You didn't wait for me?

CHARLES: How's I suppose—

CHARLOTTE: I waited for you.

> *(Silence.)*

CHARLES: Lotta good it does me now. Why'd y' sign that application form for anyways?

CHARLOTTE: To stop being lonely. *(Silence.)* How about you?

> *(Silence.)*

You spent two winters here? By yourself? How did you make out, Charles?

CHARLES: … they were … real long.

CHARLOTTE: You've been here two years. Before that, all those years with your family. Yes Charles, I am almost twice as old as you. Twice as much winter in my life. We have our winters in common. That's more than most people.

> *(Silence.)*

They tell me that come spring you're a good farmer.

CHARLES: You were talkin' around?

CHARLOTTE: A bit. *(Silence.)* Don't you want to know what they said?

CHARLES: No.

CHARLOTTE: They think you're a little crazy.

CHARLES: Like father like son.

CHARLOTTE: They say you've got schemes to—

CHARLES: Doesn't make any difference what they say.

> *(CHARLES reins in the horse. The skid of the sleigh and jangle of bells stops. Wind. Northern lights.)*

Only thing that matters is that.

CHARLOTTE: What?

CHARLES: Top 'a the rise.

CHARLOTTE: …?! That is your place?

CHARLES: Looks best in moonlight.

CHARLOTTE: A sod hut and a shed.

CHARLES: That's all she is to look at. That 'n a quarter section of broken land. Y' can't see what was gonna be there. Didn't have a chance back home. Now it looks like …

> *(Silence.)*

CHARLOTTE: Charles?

CHARLES: Everythin' out here … there's nothin' you can get yer hands on. I mean, rain, hoppers, wind, rust … prices … it can all go. Nothin' to count on.

CHARLOTTE: There is.

>   *(CHARLES gives a soft, hopeless snort.)*

Promises, Charles.

CHARLES: Promises—!

CHARLOTTE: They work if you make them work.

>   *(Silence.)*

CHARLES: I always thought when I got married …

CHARLOTTE: … that what …?

CHARLES: I dunno. I always thought y' get married in spring.

CHARLOTTE: Maybe we're winter people, Charles. We have to work through 'til spring.

>   *(Silence.)*

You want a family? I promise to try. *(Silence.)* I believe you know how?

CHARLES: I, yeah … uh, only once …

CHARLOTTE: … tell me what you see there.

>   *(CHARLES looks out at his place.)*

CHARLES: House over there. Two stories. Some a' that gingerbread stuff up around the roof. The barn over there. Dugout'll have t' be down there. Yer garden over close to it. Government'll sell me some trees real cheap. Lotsa trees.

CHARLOTTE: All that?

CHARLES: If we want it. *(Silence.)* I tried it alone. Couldn't do it.

>   *(Silence. CHARLES leans to kiss CHARLOTTE.)*

Couldn' kiss you at the ceremony, neither.

CHARLOTTE: Maybe you're not the man of the world you claim to be?

>   *(CHARLES kisses CHARLOTTE. Silence.)*

CHARLES: You must be cold. I'll take you into the house, light the stove and a lamp. I'll have to put the horse up right away. Then I'll be back in, Charlotte.

CHARLOTTE: I'll be there, Charles.

CHARLES: Let's go home.

>   *(The sleigh and winter drift away. CHARLES and CHARLOTTE go into the house. Northern lights wash into spring late afternoon.)*

RUSSELL: So everything was lovey dovey in their little dirt shack.

HAROLD: No. It took so long to get the stove and lamp lit, by time he got back outside the horse had pissed, it froze, Charles slipped on it, and threw his back out.

*(Silence.)*

RUSSELL: You're kidding.

*(Silence.)*

HAROLD: Yeah. An' y'r missin' the point about the—

RUSSELL: The point is that she promised more than she could deliver.

HAROLD: She delivered! Havin' Rachel's brother almost killed her!

RUSSELL: She hated the only living member of her family!

HAROLD: What about her promise to her husband?

RUSSELL: Look what happened: one kid died, and the other left.

HAROLD: That doesn't change her promise!

RUSSELL: The promise doesn't make any difference!

HAROLD: T' her it did! For thirty-five years she wasn't alone.

RUSSELL: Look what she turned into.

HAROLD: That's not her fault! One kid died and the other one left!

RUSSELL: You can't count on a promise! You can't even count on a contract unless you're prepared to go to court. She wouldn't have been so upset when he kicked it if she hadn't counted on him in the first place.

HAROLD: So sue her! Just what the hell else is there?

RUSSELL: Yourself. That's all you can count on.

HAROLD: Geeze, I'm real sorry you don't need help! 'Cause you'll never get any! You don't need Eva! You c'd go over to Tokyo an' be yer own wife!

RUSSELL: Put a sock in it.

HAROLD: Let's crash her! She deserves it! Let's crash everybody, eh? Crash 'em all! Me, Mrs. Teeter, yer old man! Fourteen-month-old children!

RUSSELL: What do you know about him?

HAROLD: Eva loves him. But that's okay, we're crashing her too!

RUSSELL: Back off!!

HAROLD: Why not, eh? Everybody's in this by themself. If they're right, land 'em. If they're not, crash 'em!

RUSSELL: I'm the one stuck with the kid! I'm still supportin' 'er! I'm sweating to get ahead and she's home wavin' her heels!

HAROLD: At least he's not your mistake, right?

RUSSELL: Shut up!!

HAROLD: Lucky for you it's her problem. You can just leave her!

RUSSELL: I can!! *(Silence.)* I can do that! I can leave her ... anytime and I tell you—!! All these, these, things happening and I didn't get a choice!

    *(Silence.)*

I don't know what she's been telling you but there's two sides to this.

HAROLD: Three, countin' yer kid.

RUSSELL: Is this what it's all about?! Fighting through all the ...! Why the hell did I risk my life just to have—*(Silence.)* This isn't the way I planned it.

    *(Silence.)*

The first time I saw him I swear I.... *(Silence.)* I'd just come back from looking for work overseas. I had a night home before my next flight. I wasn't going to but I figured maybe grab some clean suits.... *(Silence.)* You don't know what it's like out there. The company picnic, all the little kids runnin' around? "This is my Johnny, he plays baseball." "Little Herbie made his own kite." "This is my son Paul, he's a bastard." I know what it's like. *(Silence.)* When I used to think about it before, I swore I would never ... not after the way I was.... *(Silence.)* He woke up and he looked at me. I was so close to ... I mean, what right, how could he, how dare he! *(Silence.)* I should have left. He looked at me ... looked just like me. He doesn't look like me but—I knew what he wanted. I never had it.

HAROLD: That's not your fault. What y'r dad did.

RUSSELL: I'm doing the same thing.

HAROLD: Whose fault's that?

RUSSELL: But he's not mine!

HAROLD: Then crash 'em. It's up ahead is the bear that'll bite.

RUSSELL: I know! You're making fun of me but that is true.

HAROLD: He's a lucky kid. You're the bear.

    *(Silence.)*

RUSSELL: I don't want to hurt him.

HAROLD: Promise?

*(EVA leans against the screen door. Doesn't see RUSSELL.)*

EVA: … boy … what is in that stuff? I slept the sleep of the dead. Oh. Sorry. I don't feel that bad.

HAROLD: Where were y'?

EVA: I guess you'd call it the master bedroom.

HAROLD: What'd y' think a' the bed?

EVA: Ummm. Never slept on a thick that tick. *(Giggles.)*

RUSSELL: Would you like to go for supper?

EVA: Not really.

RUSSELL: I'm pretty hungry.

EVA: You're always hungry.

RUSSELL: Is there anyplace to get a decent meal in town?

HAROLD: Y' get home cookin' at Rita's. Y' get home cookin' at Fong's too if yer home's in Canton.

RUSSELL: Home cooking sounds great.

EVA: Russell …

RUSSELL: We could decide on the way. How far is it?

HAROLD: If yer car'll—

RUSSELL: We're walking.

HAROLD: If y' go by the road it'll take an hour. If y' cut across this field an' two a' mine y'll be there in thirty-five minutes.

RUSSELL: We'll take the road.

EVA: Russell I'm not in the mood.

RUSSELL: Let's take a break, okay?

EVA: By time we get back it's going to be…. What are we going to do?

RUSSELL: Just … have supper for a while.

*(Silence.)*

EVA: Are you going dressed like that?

RUSSELL: I, well, I'll …

HAROLD: Geeze, go into Rita's wearin' fancy stuff, they'll think yer a ballet dancer.

EVA: I was talking about the oil.

HAROLD: Oh. *(Pause.)* No one'll notice that.

RUSSELL: Let's take a break, okay?

*(Silence.)*

EVA: Okay.

*(EVA and RUSSELL walk toward the front gate. EVA stops to say something to HAROLD.)*

HAROLD: See y' tomorrow.

*(EVA heads down the hill.)*

RUSSELL: Slow down.

*(RUSSELL stops to say something to HAROLD.)*

HAROLD: The keys'll be inside. Nice meetin' you.

*(Music. RUSSELL offers his arm to EVA. She takes it. EVA and RUSSELL walk down the hill.)*

Well. Looks pretty good when they're all in, eh? Well, aside from … halfa sec'. Ah, geeze … forgot one. Had to be this guy. "Antennaria rosea." Rosy Everlasting. Looks real pretty. I don't know how it got its name. Folks I know, it takes 'em pretty much all the work they can handle t' get it t' come up. If I'm real careful I can put 'er in tomorrow.

*(HAROLD goes. Stops.)*

I always wanted t' do this. [Stage Manager's name.]?

*(The sun sets in a splendid array of gold and pink.)*

'At's swell.

*(HAROLD walks off into the sunset. The end.)*